THE BLOOMED BEAUTY

MY BEAUTY IS THE THOUGHTS BLOOMED IN ME

AMRUTHA RAVINDRAN

Contents

Contents

Contents

Preface

The papers which blotted my insights

Turn into my beauty

Now it's time to explore my footpaths

This book holds 30 poems and 80 short verses that are organized under appropriate themes. Self -publishing this book was a long and ineffable journey. A warm welcome to enjoy the taste of my art which can heal and inspire you!

Amrutha Ravindran

POEMS

1. A RELIEF

The soil devoid of water made a mourn
The sky in return returned a relieving reply
Inducing movements in the dry leaves blew the waggling wind
Darkness splashing everywhere with the sun's diminishing daylight
Opened the door for the flee of death and dryness
The drops of heaven embracing the arid areas
Thrusted into the noses the pleasing petrichor.

2. MAGICAL DROPS ON LEAVES IN THE DAWN

The chilly mornings that elucidate the obviousness of dashing to my garden

Does anyone know the incredible scene awaiting me?

Magical drops on pristine leaves looking like clear precious stones

Nearing the leaves, would I keep my eyes keen, to examine them

My hands touching them; even my fingers would tell me their ecstasy!

Would then my eyes turn into the flowers having those morning dews, gazing at them

Will be there an authentic beauty to the flowers with those outstanding drops

Being unable to keep cool, my hands longing to pluck them, unintentionally fulfilling it!!

Jiggling it above my face, I would make a slight supernatural dew drop rain

Blissful emotion felt as the drops fall on my face; way closed eyes; lips with a tremendous smile; and heart about to burst with gladness!

Then will catch my eyes the sight of lady birds rushing over the leaves, in between the bubbly drops

What if I am also a small insect alike the lady bird, being able to dash between the dews, play and enjoy on the leaves?

And would fade away to extremity those teeny-weeny water balls with the rising of the bright sun

Bare, desolate and boring would the leaves become in the absence of the magical dews, just as my mind too would be

Brings life to my just- waken soul the little dazzling lifeless drops;
remarkable vision to my eyes and immense joy to my heart!

• 7 •

3. THE MOONLIGHT OF SUNLIGHT

The sky witnessing the inevitable bond that's alive between the sun and moon

The sun shedding the brightest illumination and making the moon invisible

That action is exemplary of the sun fading to the west acquainting the appearance of the moon

Following the rising sun and vanishing moon, the bond becomes exquisite with the seldom encounter of the bonded bodies.

4. ALL NIGHTER

Far away from this world, somewhere at the vast sky, appear I, as an eye-catchy round

Warming all the hearts and providing illumination as blackness intensifies

I boast to my dazzling companions that everyone admires me

Do need to admit I that my gorgeousness remains imperfect without my glittering

neighbours near me

By indicating me, moms nourish their kids

Lend I an ear to those standing near the window, longing to share their sorrow

Would giggle I after watching those hands raising up to catch me

See I the kids slowly hitting the hay with the bed time stories about me

People going for a walk under my glistening light

Calm lakes serving as my mirrors

Animals crashing peacefully and lovely birds on the trees

Glad I am that I have been the central theme to many poems, songs and stories

People getting into a deep sleep, enjoy I looking at them

When it's time for my disappearance, to a far-flung corner I would fade away

A world with more and more selenophiles is my dream!

5. DAY TO DAWN

As I was flying high over the puffy clouds, the sun was moving beyond the horizon in the west!

Gradually was gathering darkness

Oh! The deprivation of sight by the fading sun was unfortunate

Everyone entered as if sedated into a deep crash, so was I

That absolute silence added fuel to the fire of fear in the surrounding

For a portion of the world it was resting phase

Contrastingly, the adjacent scene of the play was in the east with the rising sun above the horizon

Instantly was gathering illumination

Oh! The permission for vision by the apparent sun was fortunate

To relieve all from the profound sleep began I to hum

The chattering sound added fuel to the fire of the murmuring surrounding

For a portion of the world it was active phase

That is magnificent how the night altered to dawn...!

6. HUMAN'S NAYURE OF NATURE

What a wonder this world is?

Why does I sense this?

For the flesh and blood of nature, my sensory organs serve as witnesses

As the eternal sky is faced, likeness is felt with those who accept gladness and sadness with equilibrium

The radiant rays of the early sun represent the makers of joy in the surrounding faces

The soothing, prevailing breeze is as gentle as the serene people with calm character

As the rain shower is received with open arms, my heart does welcome those melancholic character who weeps instantly

The thunder depicts those rude natured and harsh toned people

With the arrival of the hepta-hued rainbow, all-rounders with multiple abilities are bore in mind

The non mobile solid rocks picturise those strong iron men

The saffron coloured flame burns with similar nature of the furious, bad-tempered ones

The perpetual water in seas remain phenomenal as the boundless knowledge of the intellectuals

At the moment, do you feel the feeling I feel?

It is not anything but the humans' nature of nature!

INSPIRATION

7. INVISIBLE FIRE

The fire that I have in my heart is not the fire I see through my eyes
The fire I see can be cut off but the one inside me can never be
The bronze flame causes destruction but the burning desire in me causes triumphant growth
The treacherous orange light turns everything into ashes, akin to the invisible stimulus which turns me into a phoenix
When warmth is rendered by the blazing brightness, strength is given by that fiery feeling I have!

8. A SEARCH

A long journey of excavation which began long ago with an agenda of unearthing hidden treasure of talents
That day is 'today' and that moment is 'now' he felt, as the one thousandth drop of sweat fell on the earthly ground
With an elevated heart, the treasure was unearthed which brought pride and fame!

9. A ROUTE MAP OF SUCCESS

The bare soil resembling an unknown mind
Grows there knowledge like a seed
The desire sprouting in a gentle burst
Accompanied by perseverance and diligence
As a good omen born the bud of hope
The world awoke with the bloomed results...

10. A SCOPE FOR UNITY

Not like the moon at infinity; unreachable and inaccessible

Well, it's not as the instantaneous closings and openings of eyes; easy and easier

Then what are the desires deepened in beings?

For sure the number of dreams would either be alike the glistening stars; boundless and innumerable or as countable as our fingers

Varyingly varies the varied variety of dreams!

Minuscule scope for unity among these dreams is expected if an extra dream is added to the existing ones: it's a profound longing for a morn or an eve when you vibrate your vocal cords to utter that dreams are pursued .

11. DEFEATED CALCULATIONS

Figures of plans and clouds of dreams leading to a factual beginning of something fancied

Days passing and enthusiasm losing ground; slothful laziness gaining ground

Immense interest wiping out

Kneeling down as a failed one who never made it: the intensified aim that ended in smoke

Take your eyes into the ultimate world of minor anthills which weren't made within a day

Never germinated the towering buildings from underground

And the royal palace of buzzed honey bees constructed with utmost efforts

Twigs and sticks in the beaks of birds, in a race to form their nests

Those who wrap their heads around books and becoming the wizards of knowledge

Consistency as a motive in the above mentioned ones

If the impossible is possible with a positive perspective, indeed necessary is a change for the lost aims

Grasp the goodness of devoted calculations rather than defeated calculations.

SELF DISCOVERY

12. THE POWERFUL YOU

The red rich setting sun bring forth surplus elegance to the sea brimming with beauty only for some time

Short term is the superfluous appealing look of the sky due to the ravishing moon

Not for good does the plant look prettier with its petaled bloomed flower!

Not everything can beautify your life everytime

Not everyone can beautify your life everytime

The colours to sprinkle the beauty of bliss to your life lies within the soul of you!

13. THE WEALTHY KIND

If there is kindness in your heart, that does resemble the possession of gold in your hand

With which one appears wealthier than the rich!

The wealth of gratitude which one earns with actions of gentle generosity

One who is devoid of tenderness possesses metal pieces in reality rather than gold

He is impoverished with no wealth of gratitude earned from others.

14. SOME PHOBIAS' PRO

In a mysterious solemn hour, a question was raised by one to the other: "What that could be your greatest phobia?"

"Possibly cannot be my answer a single thing; it's the atrocities of sky with lightning and thunder; the hell making high heights; eight legged spiders; and the sprightly burning fire! Attempts would never be made to try or play with them for sure," replied the other.

"It is a surety that men would stay away from his deep fears. The phenomenal fear of mine is the anxiousness about myself becoming a sinner; evil thinker; black sheep; and a despicable betrayer as Judas! It is as precise as the above mentioned surety that these fears with no doubt would make me devoid of becoming a venomous man," said the former.

With such a freaking timidity on oneself none can be as pure as gold but cannot be as poisonous as poison.

15. FOUNTAIN OF WISDOM

The knower of a larger world; with a body wholly with the essence of varied and wide-ranging lives and traditions; with unusual wings to make phenomenal flies to far flung corners; with well-shaped eyes that acts parallel to a cam for reminiscence; with heaps of rich, new tastes in his taste receptors; with the truths by his senses a fountain of wisdom is what he becomes. A traveller, is what he is addressed.

16. A MEMORABLE VISIT

When stepped into that gorgeous garden of memories, I witnessed an exemplary show of sweet smelling flowers....

Filling my hollow heart with sparkling glitters of joy, stood there the eye catchy hepta-hued bed of flowers!

The pale-white ones did bring serenity to my restless mind

The fact that the intense jet coloured flowers presented me with unappealing events cannot be denied

Proud moments flashed through my eyes after encountering those flowers of bronze colour

Then I what did I come across?

The dry drooped down flowers devoid of colour which gave me a blurry illusion!

Closed eyes wide open, lips with a gentle curve and ended I that pulchritudinous journey to the memory of memories.

17. WHAT ON OUR PLANET IS BOUNDLESS?

The nature's story that treats change as its law

The unreliable behaviour of the hardly ending sky; clear pleasant billows, swiftly turning grey

Even appearing in never predictable colours: black, blue, yellow and even red!

They eye-catching seven coloured rainbow never filled our eyesight more than a day

The sprightly burning fire once has to be extinguished

All the freshly bloomed flowers once have to be withered away

Pristine and soft leaves once have to be dried and dead

The soils once have to be changed by weathering

Never even hurricanes target a land forever

Even can't the burning, chilly or wet days remain perpetually over a land

The treasures would be unearthed by someone

The humans: greatest model of impermanence; their wretchedness and gladness won't stick to them forever!

None of us can survive mortality until that Ambrosia is discovered

Crystal clearly understood fact running in all our heads

Yet quarrels and quarrels; arrogance and arrogance; selfishness and selfishness, among the among the brightest creatures on Earth

So, what? What on Earth is durable?

The answer would be: It's change without a change, that changes everything.

18. THE PERPETUAL WORLD OF DEEPEST AFFECTION

As a new life arose from another one, formed there an everlasting world

Her life that began as a sweet daughter, lovely sister, life partner and then promoted as a care taker

Knowing no bounds held she that teeny soul in her arms, saw she an alluring world of excitement; sweet water drops with sugars of joy falling; lips nearing to that little forehead

Time passing by nurturing and pampering the little soul

Experience she sudden wake-ups at night to calm the crying soul; tender pats on that weeny shoulder leading to a deep crash

Those little footsteps along the fully developed feet touching the ground with the fully grown hands holding the little ones

Her sinking heart to fill that little tummy; fingers pointing to the crescent moon for the opening of the little mouth

Time flying and her little princess to set foot in the world of knowledge

Pride and heaps of pride felt as she dashed towards her with tokens of appreciation

Princess feeling under the weather, she whose presence blows away to far flung corner the illness

Laying on the bed, looking curiously at the top notch story teller, gradually hitting the hay with the bedtime stories

And when the bedtime stories switched into admonitions for future endeavours; galvanizing and charging her body with courage

With the dawning of day moves she heaven and earth; satisfying hearts and tummies with her secret magical ingredient

Grown up princess defying her

Perplexion increasing in that heart, giving her a piece of mind and elucidating the things to her

Despicable evil in the princess quoting these guidance as useless outrageous advices

That miserable, broken heart forgiving the unknowingness of her little sweetheart, serenely remaining with rays of hope

Ultimately the time it was to gift her princess to a prince

Heart-rending feeling it was, just as transplanting a flower from a plant

Standing by her princess through thick and thin, making her the apple of eyes continued that perpetual world of deepest affection

Many worlds as such could be seen in the single world we are in; go nowhere but to your mom and where her heart beats is the mesmerizing world of purest love ever

As a relief to our sorrow, magical fairies who effortlessly catch our inexpressible feelings

No matter how old; you will be those little playful princes and princesses in their hearts till the end....

To all the princes and princesses this is, never let those faces dim; strain every nerve for their lit-up faces!

HOPES

19. HOPEFUL STRIVE

Her two visionary stimulators were as still as a statue, with no motion
It is a prevention from the grief of someone beloved
Well, why does not those eyes restrict the instantly falling saline drops?
Not now but will nearly get back those eyes to normal circumstance;
so will her lips to a curve of smile
Though she fails to serve as an enjoyer of ecstasy at the moment but
may make it in the days yet to come
She shall strive this non-eternal melancholy.

20. THE DARK ART

The painter with a canvas painted black with no intention did not brood over the dark flop art; he took a new sheet and splashed the incredible colours. Gave he life to a charm painting.

21. HEALING LIGHT

As I took a look around, all I could see was intense blackness
All the hopes faded away
Yet, darkness was illuminated by the Almighty
Hundreds were encountered who entered into darkness
I had then the epiphany that short -lived blindness lives in everyone
Healing of the traumas is a work of God!

22. OUR GOD

Only the greatest outstanding decider, who is invisible and invincible has the accumulated power, to start and end the heart beats; for those people taking the lives of other men end up having void blessings and abundant curses!

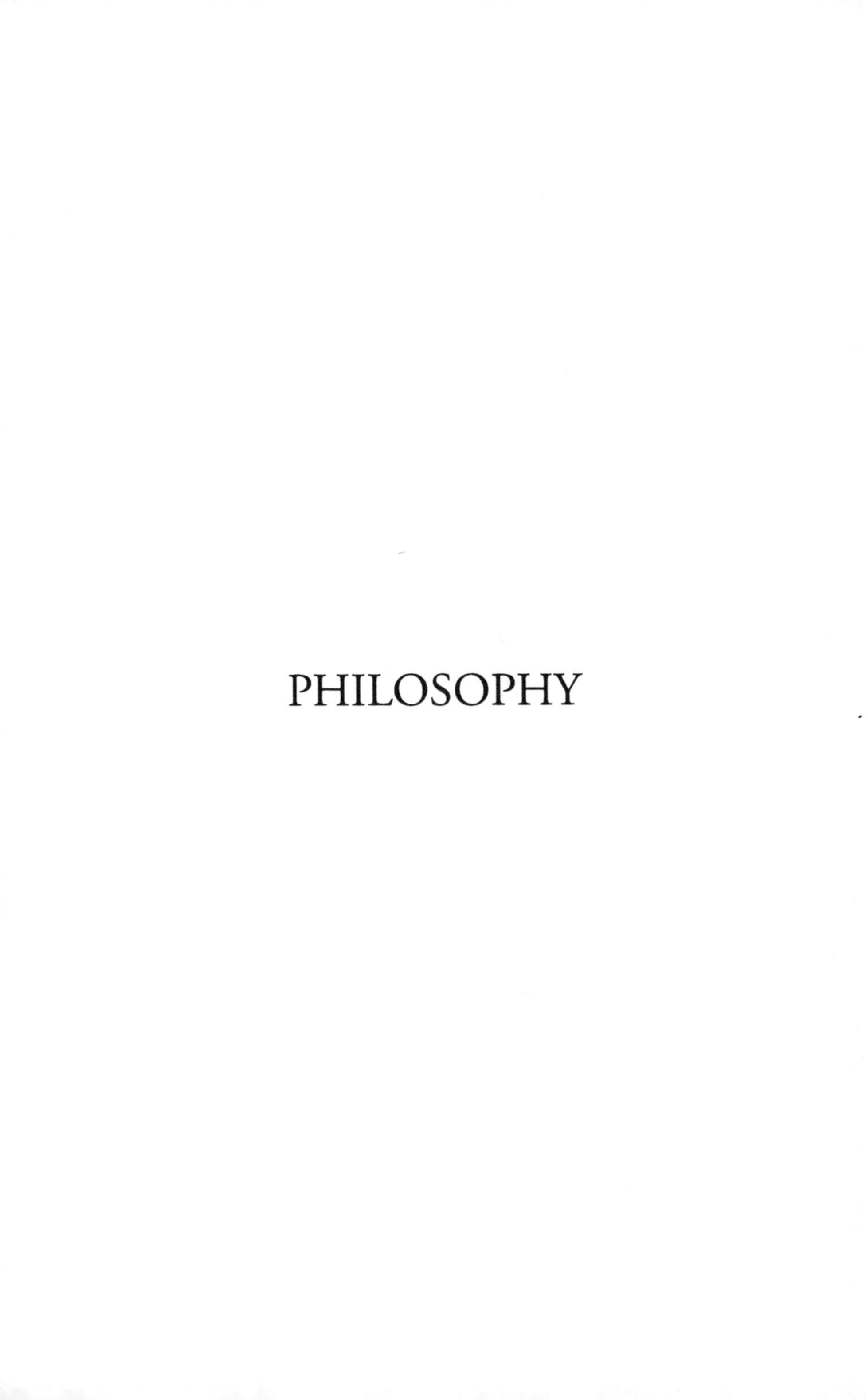

PHILOSOPHY

23. FACE OF POETRY

Poetry is a mirror showing the reflection of the poet's emotions

A knot that connects the poet's soul with the readers'

The readers digging deep to unearth the deeper roots of the transplanted experiences

The poet, an artist creating the portraits in the canvases of the readers' minds

A magician taking them to a magical world of imagination

An alchemist turning the letters of language into source of smiles.

24. THE BOXES

Once a rich man was offered a golden box which when opened contained the text "Life".

A middle-classed man was offered a silver box with "Life" written on a paper.

A poor was offered a leaden box which has the same "Life" inscribed on the paper.

Everyone is offered a life with varying circumstances alike the varying metal boxes!

25. THE LIVES TO LIVE

He who hath been living for years less in count ever since he was born on this only lively planet; what lies ahead of him is a confined ocean, satisfied with enough and more water, where he is empowered to swim and live his life of ocean, till it's water deforms to uprising vapours as his lively body amends into a lifeless one.

He who hath been living for years median in count ever since he was born on this only lively planet; what lies ahead of him is a pond with water level inferior to the former one, where he is entitled to swim and live his life of pond, till it's water deforms into uprising vapours as he becomes dead as doornail.

He who hath been living for years more when count ever since he was born on this only living planet; what lies ahead of him is just a puddle with little water prevailing where he is devoid of the power to swim and live his life, where within no time alters into vapours his life of puddle.

26. THE COMMON GIFT

A gift of chance bestowed upon all the humans

Those lead by good fortune and misfortune would open it and may find it as a rocket science

Fortunately, some rich ones beneficially absorb it; unfortunately, some never heed to it

Luckless lads would be with an intense craving for it

It is that gift of education: the opportunity to all that is used to the utmost level by lucky ones, refused by some others and can't be accessed by some poor unlucky ones.

27. A PROBLEMATIC WORLD

There exists a world of eccentric nature

What resides in there are all problems!

Essence of desperation can be deduced from their pleasing glanced appearance

We may make an entry to this world and become either a problem solver or a problem

Once conquered this world, will be there an alteration of oneself into a light hearted inventor with satisfaction

Will be you a monarch to that world of Mathematics longing for solutions

Solving the problem of problems solves the unsolved problems of one's life!!

28. MY CONCERN

How massive this universe is to hold the gigantic galaxies and substantial stars
Reserving spaces for the smallest mercury and largest Jupiter
Including the invisible radiations and visible darkness
Feeling and filling the superfluous spaces we grown on Earth
What if a reversible action occurs as opposed to the big bang theory?

ACTIVISM

29. THE ANONYMOUS KILLER

The weeny tool we used for conversation is now destroying our regular conversations

The change in it's physical appearance to a gadget with flat, smooth screen that experience our finger touches

Will anyone believe me if I say that it serves as a threat to lots of things?

Souls longing for their favourite movies and shows in the television, within a few seconds fulfilling these desires within a few finger clicks

People enjoying the beauty of their faces through it's cam but not in the mirror

Without even a shadow of doubt, the king position of books destructed by the entry of online reading

The authentic joy found in the faces of people turning the pages of their photo album and bringing back memories turned into an untruth with the memories captured by its tiny cam

The time that waits for none is now waiting for us to use it

Pushing us towards it as we make up our minds to get involved in works, converting us who fall with this pushing into lazy sloths

Having it with us, the mother nature with a drizzle cannot be enjoyed

Kids on holidays cannot be in a good bond with the nature with the hot bright sun

Killing the upcoming generation, easily injuring their capabilities, imagination and depriving their power to think

With unblinking eyes and unexpressed faces, making the rays of hope for the world smarter but not better

Taking them to the mesmerizing world of entertainment

Forcing them to stay away from ceremonies and crushing the happiness; helping them to find this lost happiness in front of that lifeless device

Getting trapped in a deep, massive hole where pleasure is found in loneliness

Killing but cruelly killing the success and joy in families

Kids refusing to heed to their parents; refusing to enjoy grandma's bedtime stories and way interested in being alone

Not only it is with the kids but also with their guiding lights

Kids craving for motherly love find mothers with their scrolling fingers in the darkness of deep creepy night or sometimes getting involved in conversing unseen characters with the gadgets near to their ears

Kids who find wretchedness with their dad's dead silence and avoidance as they long for elephant and mahout play

Cheerful conversation at the dining table, filling the whole room with sparks of joy. Now, the dropping of a pin could be heard in the dining room!

It's a precious invention of technology having myriads of advantages and disadvantages

It's an unknown truth that we all know yet we don't know that it's is a tremendous, information store and a treasure house with gigantic amount of treasures of knowledge

Thinking twice before criticising and declaring it as a killer, an answer would be found: our utilising ways caused the change of this treasure house of knowledge into a killer of our lives

Should I expect for a change in all these?

Keeping our fingers crossed let's pray and desire for a serene life!

30. A MINUSCLE IMMENSE THOUGHT IN US

A minuscule, immense thought in us, about the pureness in white and darkness in black

Impossible for a change our minds are, made with a wow for white and bad for black

Gigantically linked with the dark complexions, this colour fact

Atrociously breaking the heart of darks; stupendously warming the heart of whites

For those discriminations and refusals for black hardly anything could be done by them

Their looks built by the Almighty, with no ray of hope for a change

But nothing this sinister appearance can do if centuries are taken to wholly study a person!

Still the eyes looking into this short-term alluring faces

Stare a few minutes at the dark sky with that bright disk; history that revealed a weary rock surface behind it's dazzling charm

Light tone outside; who knows if it is dark tone inside?

Soft might be the dermis but hard might be the dermis of heart

Lovely eyes mayhap be used for atrocious views

Perfectly shaped lips most likely to be a factor for the rumours and bad mouthing

Those bonds starting with lasting impression for eyes might end with awful impression for hearts

Befriend with those who magically mesmerize you with their internal charm but not external

Do end the make-up of the visible beauty and begin the makeover for the invisible abstract beauty

May this end pave the way for a new beginning!!

SHORT VERSES

LIFE LESSONS

- Life is a beam balance where the measures happiness and sadness are inversely proportional.

- Genuine smile appears on a face due to happiness just like a rainbow that appears in the sky due to rain!

- Effectively changed world is followed by profoundly understanding the current world.

- The more conceptualized you are, the more clarified you are about the concepts of this world.

Chapter31

- Hate is a fate, faced in a bate!

- Unfavourable fates frustrate frivolity.

- What causes temporariness is the ending.

- Repetitive manner of mistakes is more monstrous than mistakes!!

Chapter32

- Excess leads to Exploitation.

- The ending process is a never-ending process.

FRIENDSHIPS & BONDS

- Being special is not so common; being common is not so special!

- Deepest ones make the deepest wounds.

- Great distance doesn't discontinue great friendship.

- The dependent moon far from the Earth elucidates that nobody on the Earth is independent.

Chapter33

- True friendship is like a homogenous mixture where separation is difficult after combination.

- Finding a trustworthy person is as difficult as finding a jewel from earth's interior; once you find both, you'll value them to the utmost level.

- Stones that are dense go deep inside the water when entered, likewise memories with deep ones that are heavy go deep inside our heart when entered.

- Some people come into your life as an unexpected summer rain, turning into an exceptional rainbow!

Chapter34

- Some people are like inevitable zeros which deforms a thousand to lakh; seems non-crucial but become quintessential when added.

- There will be a paradise of pleasure when my pleasure becomes your pleasure and your pleasure becomes mine.

EMOTIONS

- The mirror of trust when broken can hurt!

- Painful it is when the one who heals pains becomes a pain.

- Parting is difficult only when you are attached.

- Soaking the sorrows the sun sets; making the minds majestic the moon moves.

Chapter35

- If you get emotionally attached, you will be emotionally damaged!

- The pain given by your foe can make you down; the pain given by your friend can break you down!

- The one who's enriched with memorable memories feels coupled ecstasy and misery while the one who lost them feels emptiness!

- Naturally, nature of emotions nurture the nature of memories.

Chapter36

- The way situations behave changes that way we behave.

- Getting old is alike the blinking of eyes which happens instantly without much of our awareness!

- Remove the darkness of dissatisfaction with the illumination of blessings.

- At times, the journey is more enjoyed than the destination.

- It's a beautiful blessing to be blessed with bliss.

INSIGHTS

- It's change without a change that changes everything.

- Trust is a tool to measure the depth of friendship.

- Intense insights can identify elegant evils.

- To use the useful is better than not using it; to not use the useful is way better than misusing it!

Chapter37

- The extension of our experience may not reach the exaggeration of their expression!

- Cross all the limits to not cross your limits.

- Man deprives time from having excess hours in a day. Time deprives man from the use of excess hours in a day.

- What most to be expected is to be least in expecting.

Chapter38

- The knowledge roots of a teacher are like the wine which strengthens with passage of time!

- The instances to elucidate the catastrophic clashes of contradictions can be inferred from the misery that ceases ecstasy, atrocities that win over generosities and darkness that fades light.

- The candle of the world providing the brightest illumination brings water to our eyes when looked at with adoring admiration!

- Those fond of exclusion find excuses.

Chapter39

- At times, we don't need sufficient time but the ability to use time sufficiently.

- A search for easiness may result in the discovery of hardness.

- Arrogance results in repulsion with the rest.

PERSONAL GROWTH

- Let yourself to be yourself, so you don't let yourself down by yourself.

- Manners are magnets which attract minds.

- What defines you is how you define you.

- To be happy for your victory is common, but for others' is not.

Chapter 40

- To control what's out of your control is not under your control.

- Laziness is not a rare disorder that affects one in a million but a common disorder that affects a million.

- The mirror shows who knows you the best in this world.

- Fear pulls you towards your comfort zone.

Chapter 41

- Do not let the darkness of the night take over the brightness of the dawn.

- Consistency is not a common calibre but a common concern.

- Though we are not capable of doing everything, we all are capable of doing something.

- What already happened is just a story that's likely to be told. What's happening is the reality in which we must live. What's going to happen is just a blurry illusion that can't be foreseen.

Chapter42

- If you fail in front of failure, you will fail in front of success.

- Give up the act of giving up.

- Overcome the resistances offered by life to your journey throughout it!

- The biggest fools are the ones who fool themselves.

Chapter43

- An inglorious past can destroy a glorious present; a glorious past cannot destroy an inglorious present!

- Readers walk following the footpaths of writers!

- A beautiful behaviour beautifies a being.

- Progress in making progress to be more progressed.